D0429192

KEEKER

and the Sneaky Pony

KEEKER

and the Sneaky Pony

by **HADLEY HIGGINSON** Illustrated by **MAJA ANDERSEN**

chronicle books · san francisco

Book design by Kristine Brogno and Mary Beth Fiorentino.
Typeset in Weiss Medium.
The illustrations in this book were rendered in pen and ink and
then digitally textured.
Manufactured in China.

Library of Congress Cataloging-in-Publication Data
Higginson, Hadley.
Keeker and the sneaky pony / by Hadley Higginson ; illustrated by
Maja Andersen.
p. cm.
Summary: When eight-year-old Keeker gets a pony, she is faced
with the challenge of winning the animal's trust and friendship,
and they both come to understand the phrase "You scratch my
back and I'll scratch yours."
ISBN-13: 978-0-8118-4052-1 (library edition)
ISBN-10: 0-8118-4052-2 (library edition)
ISBN-13: 978-0-8118-5217-3 (pbk.)
ISBN-10: 0-8118-5217-2 (pbk.)
[1. Ponies—Fiction. 2. Horsemanship—Fiction. 3. Trust—Fiction.]
I. Andersen, Maja, ill. II. Title.
PZ7.H534945Kee 2006
[E]—dc22
2005012065

Distributed in Canada by Raincoast Books
9050 Shaughnessy Street, Vancouver, British Columbia V6P 6E5

10 9 8 7 6 5 4 3 2

Chronicle Books LLC
85 Second Street, San Francisco, California 94105

www.chroniclekids.com

Dedicated to my parents, who gave me the perfect wild and woolly childhood —Hadley Higginson

To Kai, Tom and Cecil —Maja Andersen

Chapter 1

This is Catherine Corey Keegan Dana, but everyone calls her Keeker. Keeker is eight. She lives in the country with her mother, her father, five dogs, two cats, a goat and a parakeet. She loves all the pets, of course, but not one of them is really "hers." She'd like someone to go around with and tell things to. What she really wants is a pony.

This is Plum. Plum is a Shetland pony who lives in a big field at Berry Hill Farm.

She likes to canter around with the other ponies, snorting at butterflies.

She rarely, if ever, thinks about little girls. She certainly doesn't want one.

This is how Keeker and Plum met. One day while Plum was busy cantering and snorting, a

big rig pulled into the driveway at Berry Hill.
It was a truck with a horse trailer. The farmer
who owned Plum led her out of the field and
tried to coax her into the trailer.

But the trailer was dark and scary and
smelled funny. Plus, it rattled and clanked.

"Yikes," thought Plum. "I'm not getting on
that thing!"

The farmer talked to Plum gently. He fed her
some carrots and showed her that there were
more in the trailer if she would just walk up the
ramp.

Plum was exceedingly fond of carrots. So
she put one foot on the ramp, then another,
then another. . . .

That same day not so very far away, Keeker was sitting outside her house, feeling sad.

Even though she took riding lessons every week AND went to riding camp every summer AND had read a kazillion books on horses and horse care, it still seemed as though she would never, ever get her own pony.

"BOY am I sad," thought Keeker. She wasn't sure whether she looked as sad as she felt, though, so she tried to make her eyes fill up with tears.

It was hard to do. So hard she almost didn't notice the big truck coming down the road, headed right for the Danas' house.

The truck with a horse trailer pulled into Keeker's yard, and Keeker's mom came whizzing out of the house to help the driver unload the trailer.

Plum came clattering down the ramp.

"I had a pony when I was your age," said Keeker's mom, "and now you have one, too. Congratulations!"

Keeker stared at Plum.

"My OWN pony," thought Keeker. "I love her already."

Plum stared at Keeker.

"Whose girl is this?" thought Plum.

Keeker wanted to go riding right away, but her mom said no—not until Plum got used to her new home.

Plum appeared to be quite comfortable. So comfortable, in fact, that all she did was eat. *Munch, munch, munch.*

Keeker liked to sit cross-legged in the field and watch Plum's rubbery lips move around in the grass.

"What a nosy little girl," grumped Plum. "I wish she would go away and let me eat in peace."

Chapter

2

Finally, FINALLY, it was riding day. When Keeker woke up that morning, it felt like Christmas. Even the dogs were running around barking crazily, as if they knew something great was about to happen.

Keeker got dressed and hurried to the field to get Plum.

Plum let her get close, then trotted off.

When Keeker slowed down, Plum slowed down.

When Keeker sped up, Plum sped up.

"Rats!" said Keeker. "This pony is sneaky!"

Keeker tried showing her who was boss.

"PLUM! GET OVER HERE!"

Keeker tried coaxing her with a carrot.

"Heeeeere ponyponypony."

"That pony is IMPOSSIBLE!"

Keeker was so frustrated that there was only one thing left to do. So she went behind the barn to stomp around and cry a little.

"What a silly girl," sighed Plum. "All she had to do was ask nicely."

Plum wandered off to look for clover blossoms.

After her temper tantrum, Keeker felt better. She found her parents and asked for their help. Keeker's father went into the field and spoke nicely to Plum, who allowed herself to be caught and led into the barn.

Keeker's mom and dad helped Keeker brush her off and put on the brand-new saddle and bridle.

Plum saw her reflection in the tractor and snorted.

"Who's THAT?"

Keeker and Plum were ready for their ride.

"Just go to the end of the road, then come

back," said Keeker's mom. "If you want, I'll go

with you. I can guide Plum on the lead rope."

"NO!" said Keeker. "I want to go by myself."

After all, she was an experienced rider. Lead

ropes were for babies.

Chapter

3

Keeker and Plum set off down the road at a fast walk—*clop-clop*. It was a lovely bird-sing-y, sun-zing-y day, and Plum felt frisky.

So frisky, in fact, that she started going faster—*cloppity-clop*. Soon she was trotting—*cloppity-cloppity-clop*.

Keeker held tight to Plum's mane, so she wouldn't fall off. She'd never been jiggled so

hard in her life. It felt as if all her brains were going to bounce loose.

"Enough of this," Keeker thought.

"WHOA!" she said, and Plum stopped. They were about a mile down the road, right at the place where Keeker's mom had said to turn around.

Off to the left was a little trail that went winding into the woods.

"THAT looks interesting," thought Plum. She flicked one ear back to see what Keeker thought.

Keeker wasn't sure. She knew they were
supposed to turn around, but she'd been on
that trail before, with her mom, and she knew
where it went.

"Okay," Keeker said. She gave Plum a little kick.

They headed into the woods, following the trail.

Once they were in the woods, it was like
being in a whole different world. *Swish-swoosh-
swish,* Keeker and Plum plowed through the
tall ferns. Birds chittered and hooted over-
head. Squirrels raced around. The whole forest
seemed to be moving.

Plum put her nose in the air and took big sniffs.
She smelled lots of good things to eat—moss and
nuts and roots and curled-up little fiddleheads.

"I might need to lose this girl," thought Plum
sneakily, "so I can really enjoy these woods."

Just then a fat chipmunk came racing down the path, headed right for Plum's two front hooves.

"Yippee!" thought Plum. "Here's my chance."

She bugged her eyes out and snorted and reared up. Keeker slid off backwards and landed on her bottom in the dirt.

"Oooooo, oooooo, I am so SCARED of chipmunks!" pretended Plum as she cantered off.

Keeker was all alone in the woods.

Chapter

4

"Rats," said Keeker. Plum had charged off into the ferns, and Keeker had no choice but to follow her. Even though the forest seemed bigger and darker than it had before, and the noises didn't sound quite so friendly.

Keeker set off to find her pony.

Swish-swish. Clomp-clomp. Keeker walked and walked and walked, but still no Plum.

Finally, she sat down on a stump to have a rest. Her feet hurt, and she had bugs in her hair, and she was as tired and thirsty as she had ever been. Everything was horrible.

"Maybe I'll never find my way home," thought Keeker sadly. She began to think of everything she would miss: her mom, her dad, the goat, the dogs, blueberry pancakes, presents, making things with glue and tape—the list was endless.

She let her eyes fill up with tears a little. She thought about stomping and crying, but there didn't seem to be much point. Instead, she lay down in the moss and had a think. She tried to put herself in Plum's shoes.

"If I were a sneaky pony," Keeker wondered, "where would I go?"

Suddenly, she knew. She remembered a place farther up the trail that opened onto a clearing, a place with tall grass and lots of blackberries.

"That pony is a P-I-G! If she got back on the trail ahead of me, I bet that's where she went!"

Chapter

5

Keeker raced back the way she'd come, found the trail and hurried up it. She burst onto the clearing, and there was Plum, standing in a blackberry bramble.

Plum was covered in purple smudges, and her saddle was crooked. She looked grumpy.

Keeker ran to try to catch her, and Plum ran away, dragging bits of blackberry bush with her.

This went on for a while.

"Why can't I catch her?" moaned Keeker. She was almost ready to cry again. But she didn't. Instead, she sat down and thought some more. She remembered something her father had said, something about "I'll scratch your back if you'll scratch mine."

Then she had an idea. She ran off to find the perfect scratching stick. Then, she started walking verrrrry slowly towards Plum.

"What's she up to?" thought Plum. She kept one eye on the berry she was nibbling, one eye on Keeker.

Keeker got closer

and closer

and closer,

until she was only a few feet away.

Keeker reached out with the stick and began to scratch. Plum was a little startled, but then the scratching began to feel really good. Especially since she was covered in burrs and blackberry goo and was probably the itchiest she'd ever been in her whole life.

"Oooooooooooooo, I like this girrrrrrrrrrlllllll," sighed Plum as she leaned into the delicious scratching. She wiggled her lip and swished her tail. Keeker scratched and scratched and scratched.

Finally, when all her itches had been scratched, Plum walked over and put her head against Keeker's chest.

She was a tired pony. She missed her new home, with the dogs and the goat and apples and dinnertime. She even missed the old bathtub she drank her water out of.

She wanted to go home. And so did Keeker. Plum sighed a big sigh and let Keeker hop onto her back.

Chapter

6

Keeker and Plum got back on the trail, heading towards the road.

On the way home, Plum didn't bounce or jiggle Keeker at all. In fact, she walked very carefully, trying not to scrape Keeker's knees on the trees.

Keeker used a branch to swat the flies away from Plum's ears.

When they got home, Keeker's parents were VERY glad to see them.

Keeker's mom gave Plum a molasses mash for dinner, and Keeker had hot dogs with no bun, just the way she liked them.

Keeker went to bed early. But before she crawled under the covers, she popped her head out the window to take one last look at the night. She could see Plum in her paddock, drinking from her tub. (Of course, Plum wasn't really drinking—she was bubble-blowing.)

"I'm glad I got a girl," thought Plum as she burbled away. "With a little more training, she'll be just right."

Plum wandered over to the apple tree to lie down. She fell asleep right away, dreaming about blackberries. Up in her bedroom, Keeker dreamed she had ferns instead of hair.

The night was long and dark and purply. It lasted all the way until morning.

 Pony Facts

Ponies are not short horses or baby horses; they are their own separate breed. Ponies do not grow to be big like horses—they stay small. Ponies are frisky and love to play with other ponies. They are also known for being sneaky and sometimes play tricks on their owners and the other ponies they live with.

Ponies are wonderful pets, but it takes lots of time and work to take good care of them. Ponies are fun to ride. Some people even show their ponies at horse shows and win ribbons.

Just like dogs, ponies have to get regular care from veterinarians or animal doctors.

They even have to go to the dentist. Hoof care is also important for ponies. A pony's hooves should be cleaned every day to keep them healthy.

A pony's height is measured in "hands." One "hand" is 4 inches long. To measure a pony's height, measure from the ground by the pony's front hoof to the bump at the top of the pony's back. Then divide the total number of inches by four to get the number of "hands" the pony is.

Most adult ponies weigh between 400 and 700 pounds. A pony's weight can be measured with a special tape measure that goes around its stomach and measures in pounds instead of inches.

Mama ponies or "mares" are very protective of their babies or "foals." Sometimes they run and play with their babies and other times they graze, while their babies sleep nearby.

A pregnant mare carries her foal for 11 months before giving birth. A brand-new foal can stand on its wobbly legs within 20 minutes after it is born. This is necessary so it can quickly reach its mother's milk.

Foals grow quickly and soon learn to eat grass, hay and grain. Ponies also love to eat treats like carrots and apples.

Hadley Higginson grew up on a farm in Vermont where she had a sneaky pony of her own. She lives in Atlanta where she works as a writer for an advertising firm.

Although she currently has no pony, she does have a bossy little dog. This is her first book.

GALLOPING YOUR WAY IN FALL 2006

Introducing two new adventures in the Sneaky Pony series

KEEKER
and the Horse Show Show-Off

The adventures of Keeker and her pony sidekick, Plum, continue as they take to the ring in their very first horse show. Keeker and Plum have discovered that they love to jump—over hay bales, over watering cans, over almost anything. When a flyer arrives announcing an upcoming horse show, Keeker is sure they should enter. Plum practices flaring her nostrils to look like a wild horse. Keeker practices her acceptance speech for when she wins the blue ribbon. But when they arrive at the ring and meet horse-show veteran Tifni and her fancy pony, Lulu's Li'l Windsong, the real challenge begins.

KEEKER
and the Sugar Shack

It's mud season in Vermont, and everyone has cabin fever. Keeker is so bored that she has started wearing pantyhose on her head to pretend she has long braids. So when she learns that an old woman has bought the run-down Crabapple Farm, she decides she and Plum need to go investigate. Along the way, the two detectives befriend their eccentric neighbor (and her huge dog, Clancy) and learn that even mud season can be magical when you're making maple syrup.